# Water, Water, Everywhere

CONTENTS

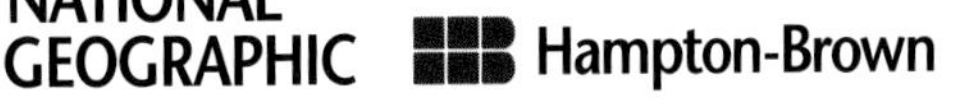

School Publishing

# Words with u_e

Look at each picture. Read the words.

**Example:**

mule

commute

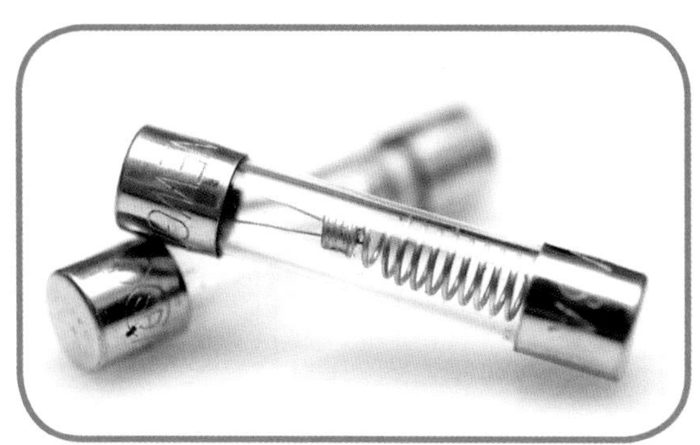

fuse

volume

| High Frequency Words |
|---|
| city |
| hold |
| land |
| mile |
| much |
| river |
| sea |
| wash |

# Key Words

Look at the picture. Read the sentences.

**A Trip on a Ship**

1. People ride a ship down the **river**.
2. They go out on the **sea** for a trip.
3. They go for **miles** and miles.
4. They do not see a **city** or **land** for **much** of the trip.
5. The waves **wash** on the side of the ship.
6. If the waves get big, the people must **hold** on.

What would you like to see from a ship?

Phonics Games

NGReach.com

# How Can We Use Water?

by Anna Halloran

People use water in lots of ways. They have invented ways to stop water, hold water, and save water. Then they can use it for fun, to drink, to be safe, and more!

One way to save water is to put up a dam. A dam will hold back a river.

When water is saved in back of a dam, it can form a lake miles long. People can swim or ride boats in this lake.

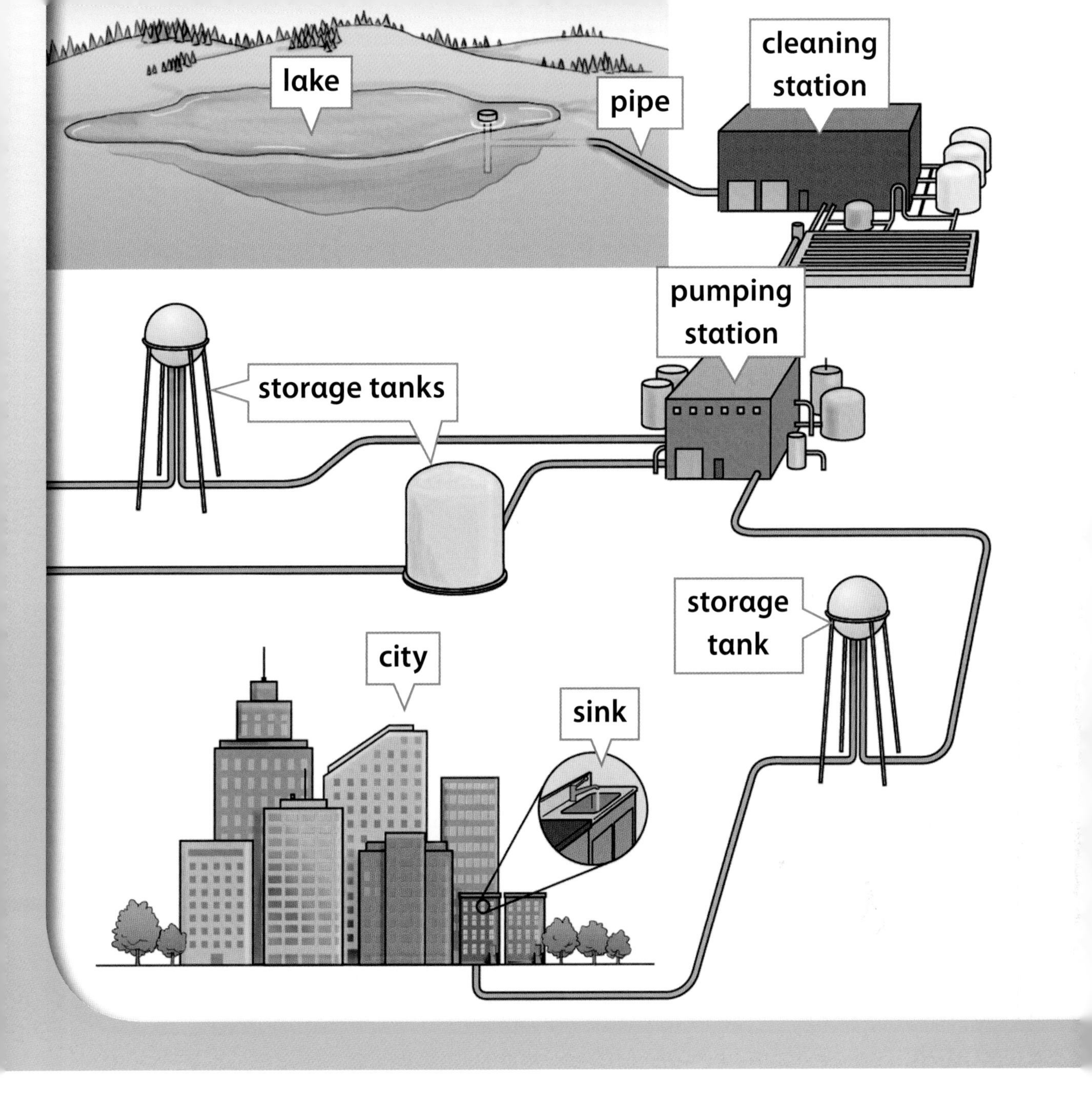


Or the water from such a lake can be sent to a city. Then people will have water for drinking, washing, and other uses.

One way to stop flooding is to put up a dike. A dike will hold back the sea or a lake. This stops water from flooding the land in back of the dike.

A lock can help boats use a river in which the water level shifts up and down.

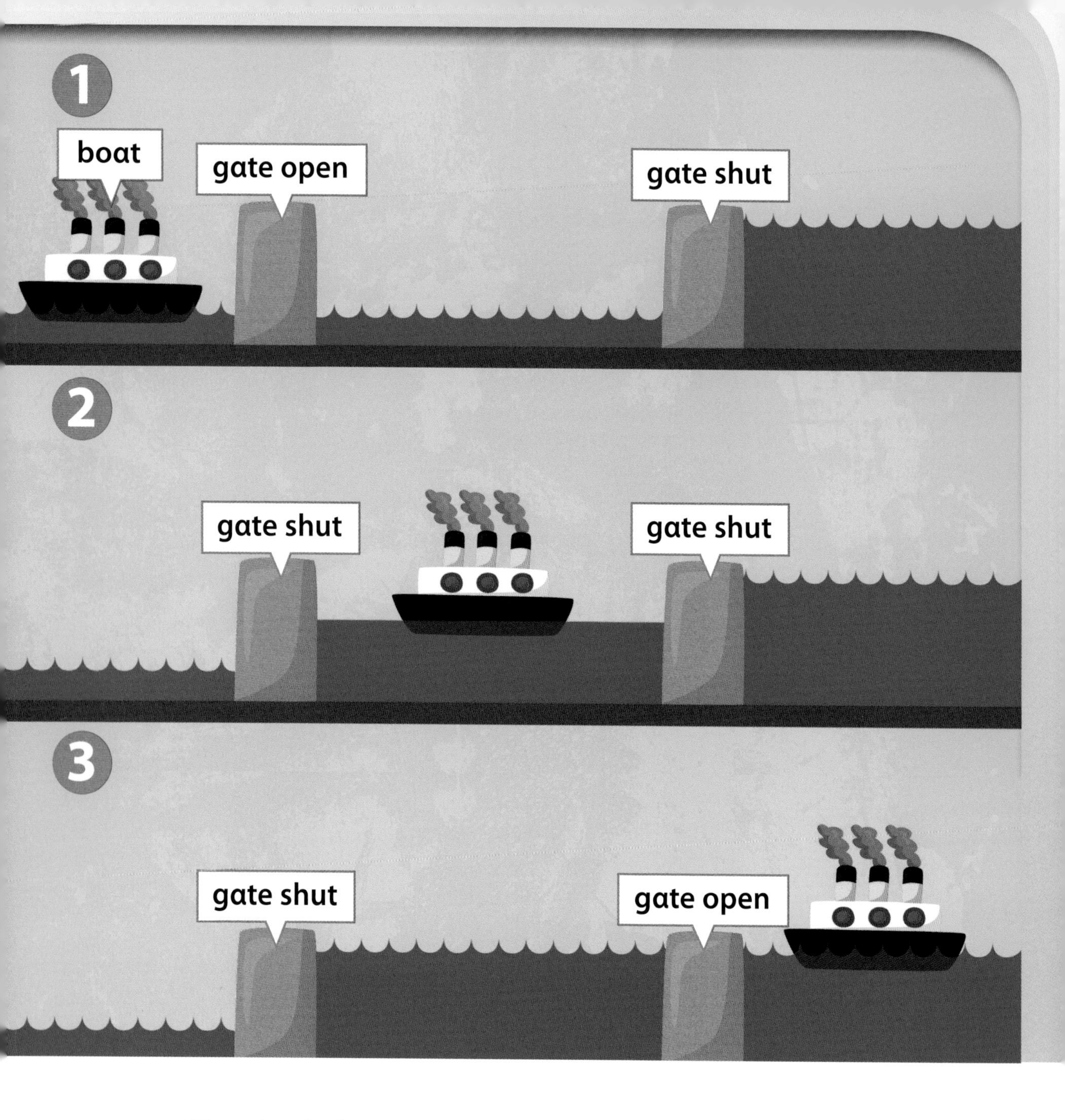


The lock has gates at each end. It has a way to let water in and out. The water can lift boats up and drop them down.

In the past, mules were used to tug boats through the lock. Now boats go through without using mules.

Some people commute, or go from home to jobs, on water. They take a boat to get to jobs.

Some people take fun trips on boats. They can eat on these boats. They can even ski off these boats!

People *can* use water in lots of ways.

# Words with u_e

Read these words.

| | | | |
|---|---|---|---|
| mule | drink | use | cube |
| hat | box | fuse | cute |

Find the words with long **u**.
Use letters to build them.

m u l e

**Talk Together**

Choose words from the box to tell your partner about the pictures.

**1.**

**2.**

**3.**

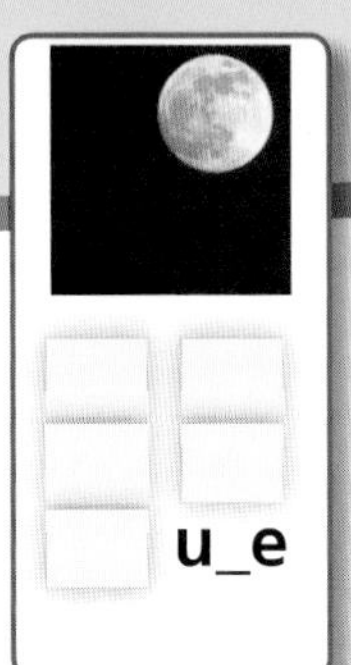


# More Words with u_e

Look at each picture. Read the words.

Example:

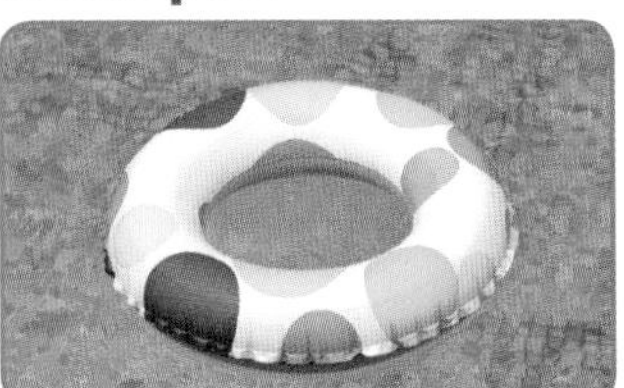

tube

prune

dune

costume

June

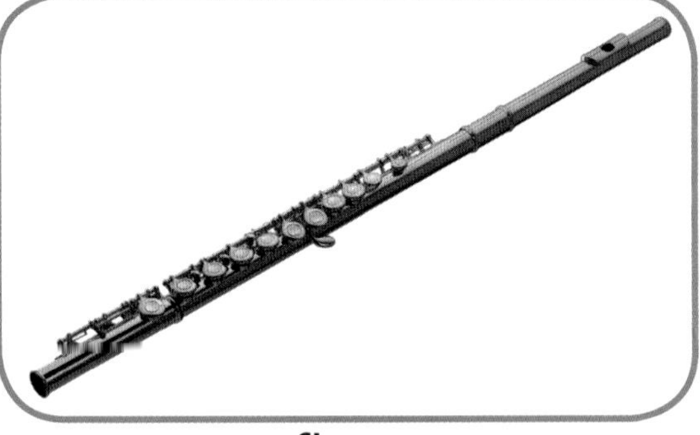

flute

| High Frequency Words |
| --- |
| city |
| hold |
| land |
| mile |
| much |
| river |
| sea |
| wash |

# Key Words

Look at the picture. Read the sentences.

**City Water**

1. People live in a **city** by the **sea**.
2. How can they get fresh water to drink and **wash** with?
3. The water could come from a **river**.
4. It could come from a lake **miles** away.
5. The water passes through pipes under the **land**.
6. The city sets up tanks to **hold** **much** of its water.

# Our Planet's Water

by Ryan Fadus

Can you name a body of water? Our planet includes lots of them. These are just some.

An ocean is the biggest body of water. There are five oceans on this planet.

At the ocean, we can swim and sail. On a hot June day, people will fill the beach.

We must stick to the rules. The rules include swimming in the flag zone and not walking on the dunes.

A sea is a big body of water that has land on all or most of its sides. It can be included as part of an ocean.

A gulf is a big inlet of the ocean. Much of a gulf is enclosed by land. Because the land protects the water, a gulf is a safe spot for boats to dock.

We can visit a city on a gulf. Some people are dressed in costumes. They make tunes with flutes.

A river is a long body of running fresh water. It spills into the sea or other body of water. A river can run for miles.

We can ride tubes down a river. Rapids make the ride super fun.

A creek is a little body of running fresh water. It can run into a river and add its water to the river.

A lake is a big body of fresh water enclosed by land. We can swim, sail, and fish at a lake.

# More Words with u_e

Read these words.

| flute | rule | ride | dune |
|---|---|---|---|
| raft | June | hike | tube |

Find the words with **u_e**.
Use letters to build them.

f l u t e

**Talk Together**

Choose words from the box to tell your partner about things to do by or on water.

Take a hike on a dune.

1.

2.

3.

# Beach City Puzzle

The signs in Beach City are missing letters. Work with a partner to fix the signs. Use the word clues on page 31.

Word Clues
dune
sea
River
Costume
Tube
More
Flutes
Hold
Rule
wash
June
Mule
Computer
Rule
C _ m _ _ _ _ _
Store
C_ _ t_ _ _ Shop
SOAP
We _ _ sh too!
Rent a _u_ _.
R_ _ e Number One
H _ _ _ on tight!
Red _ i _ _ r

**Acknowledgments**
Grateful acknowledgment is given to the authors, artists, photographers, museums, publishers, and agents for permission to reprint copyrighted material. Every effort has been made to secure the appropriate permission. If any omissions have been made or if corrections are required, please contact the Publisher.

**Photographic Credits**
**CVR** Epic Stock/Shutterstock. **2** (bl) Elena Aliaga/Shutterstock. (br inset) G.K. & Vikki Hart/ Photodisc/Getty Images. (brc) George Doyle/Getty Images. (cl) Studio 37/Shutterstock. (tl) Michael Klenetsky/iStockphoto. (trc) John A. Rizzo/Getty Images. **3** (b) Liz Garza Williams/Hampton-Brown/ National Geographic School Publishing. (t) Tool Using Animal/Shutterstock. **4** Corbis Super RF/Alamy Images. **5** Patrick Eden/Alamy Images. **6** Getty Images/Jupiterimages. **8** Bloomberg via Getty Images. **9** Kip Ross/National Geographic Image Collection. **11** Science & Society Picture Library/Getty Images. **12** Frank VandenBergh/iStockphoto. **13** Thomas Duncan/Imagestate. **14** Blend Images/SuperStock. **15** Liz Garza Williams/Hampton-Brown/National Geographic School Publishing. **16** (bl) Alex Slobodkin/iStockphoto. (br) Artville. (brc) Jupiterimages. (cl) Polka Dot Images/Jupiterimages. (tl) Cristiano Pereira Ribeiro/Shutterstock. (trc) Michael Hill/iStockphoto. **17** (b) Liz Garza Williams/Hampton-Brown/National Geographic School Publishing. (t) David Young-Wolff/PhotoEdit. **18-19** Goodshoot/Jupiterimages. **20** B. Anthony Stewart/National Geographic Image Collection. **21** INSADCO Photography/Alamy Images. **22** James Forte/National Geographic Image Collection. **23** gkuna/Shutterstock. **24** Grant Rooney/Alamy Images. **25** John Stanmeyer/ National Geographic Image Collection. **26** Kevin Schafer/Danita Delimont/Alamy Images. **27** John Foxx Images/Imagestate. **28** Peter Brogden/Alamy Images. **29** Liz Garza Williams/Hampton-Brown/ National Geographic School Publishing.

**Illustrator Credits**
**7** Dartmouth Publishing; **10**, **15**, **19**, **29** Jannie Ho; **30-31** Vanessa Newton



National Geographic School Publishing
Hampton-Brown
www.NGSP.com

RR Donnelley, Jefferson City, MO

ISBN: 978-0-7362-8067-9

12 13 14 15 16 17 18 19
10 9 8 7 6 5 4